AF808005

Presented to July04

Alicia

From

Keystone Neighbors

A GIFT OF

Sunshine for a Friend's Heart

Stories for the Heart® *Mini* Books

COMPILED *by* ALICE GRAY

Multnomah Gifts™
Multnomah® Publishers Sisters, Oregon

A Gift of Sunshine for a Friend's Heart

a Stories for the Heart *Mini* Book

published by Multnomah Gifts™, a division of Multnomah® Publishers, Inc.
P.O. Box 1720, Sisters, Oregon 97759

ISBN 1-59052-025-4

Designed by Koechel Peterson & Associates, Minneapolis, Minnesota

Multnomah Publishers, Inc., has made every effort to trace the ownership of all poems and quotes. In the event of a question arising from the use of a poem or quote, we regret any error made and will be pleased to make the necessary correction in future editions of this book.

Please see the acknowledgments at the back of the book for complete attributions for this material.

Printed in China

03 04 05 06 07 08—10 9 8 7 6 5 4 3 2 1

www.multnomahgifts.com

Table of Contents

Morning Walk

Author unknown

Six a.m. Two women in windsuits are out for their morning walk. As they walk, they talk about their important friendships: husbands, kids, coworkers. They occasionally touch each other's shoulders, stop, face each other, and laugh. A sun-dried seventy-something man, wearing a neon orange ski hat, walks by, smiles, and says, "You two look like you're doing ballet together." And so they are. As friends, they are dancing in synchrony: listening, encouraging, challenging each other.

Friendship is the essence and
aroma of life, distilled from
human hearts that find
in each other the understanding
of the other's needs. It is the
understanding that opens wide
the doors of friendship and lets
the heart pass through.

EDWIN OSGOOD GROVER

Every true
friend is
a glimpse of God.

LUCY LARCOM

CeCe and Agnes

Mary Treacy O'Keefe

Cecelia and Agnes did not become good friends until many years after they met. Cecelia was nearly ten years older than Agnes, so they did not know each other despite living in the same rural community. Their relationship began as in-laws, brought together when Cecelia's daughter married Agnes's son. Later, after both women's husbands died, they became closer than ever, conversing several times each week and often traveling together.

In the early years of their friendship, Cecelia and Agnes saw each other mainly at family gatherings. They loved attending the various celebratory events of their children's lives. Birthdays, anniversaries, and the holidays were times of shared happiness. After the deaths of their husbands, Agnes and Cecelia consoled each other in their grief and eventually became the best of friends. They watched with pride as their children became grandparents, and every new addition to their families brought more joy. As their families became more independent, Cecelia and Agnes ventured beyond their small midwestern hometown and explored the United States together.

After many years of enjoying each other's company, the years finally took their toll on Cecelia. As the older woman approached her mideighties, her mind became more and more confused. Cecelia's family eventually had to make the difficult decision to move her to a nursing home. Agnes, on the other hand, remained as busy as ever, her mind sharp and her wit quick.

A true friend, Agnes was determined to help Cecelia however she could, especially on her almost daily visits to her friend in the nursing home. For several years beyond the time when Cecelia could recognize her, Agnes kept coming to see and talk to "Cece." As Agnes approached her eighties, she wondered why Cece continued to live, it seemed, long past her prime. She commented frequently to the nurses at the home, "God must have forgotten my friend Cece. If I go first, I will tell Him to go and get her and bring her straight to heaven!" Everyone laughed, never dreaming that Agnes—a picture of health herself—would go first.

But Agnes did die first, one frigid December morning, without warning to her many friends and family members. The family was devastated at this unexpected shock. Agnes's funeral was delayed for several days since the weather was so cold and the ground was frozen solid.

Finally, the family was able to gather to celebrate Agnes's life. As her son and daughter-in-law prepared to leave for the church, they received a call from the nursing home informing them that their children's other grandmother, Cecelia, had just passed away.

As the news of Cecelia's death spread throughout the church during Agnes's funeral, one might have been surprised to see smiles and hear a few chuckles at such a sad event. Yet those who knew the two women well and had heard Agnes's promise to "talk to God" if she got to heaven first were immediately consoled in their grief. The two best friends were together again at last, joined with their Creator and each other forever.

Friendship...is like the beautiful
shadows of evening.
Spreading and growing till life
and its light pass away.

MICHAEL VITKOVICS

Treat Your Friends

Treat your friends always
as if you had all the time
in the world to enjoy them.
But remember that it's
the smallest moments
which often matter most.

HEATHER HARPHAM KOPP

The Crazy Quilt

Melody Carlson

I have an old quilt made by my father's grandmother. It's not a beautiful quilt, and all the fabric appears to be quite old. But I love it.

The pieces are probably leftover scraps from Aunt Fran's apron, little Mary's Easter dress, or Grandpa's favorite shirt. They are odd shapes and sizes. Some nameless shapes have hooks and curves, long slivers of fabric painstakingly sewn with dozens of meticulous stitches. A few tiny patches are smaller than my thumbnail.

Some of the fabric is very plain with dull color. I can just hear some tired mother say, "But, dear, it's a very serviceable cloth..." while her daughter frowns at the new school dress. Other pieces are bright and cheery, like snippets of birthdays, summer vacations, and fun times gone by. A few fancier pieces are satiny smooth with embossing or embroidery; they seem to whisper of weddings, dances, a first kiss....

My father's grandmother was nearly blind and perhaps that explains why the shades appear haphazardly arranged and almost seem to shout at each other. I wonder if she ever realized what her creations looked like, or did she simply go by touch? They do have an interesting texture—smooth next to bumpy, seersucker alongside velvet. And all over the quilt, hundreds of tiny stitches, almost invisible to the eye, pucker ever so slightly.

If I were blind, I would like to make quilts like this.

Recently my own family relocated to a new town, and I was in bed with the flu, wrapped in my great-grandmother's crazy quilt. I felt sorry for myself and I missed the friends I'd left behind. Deep down, I knew it was partly my own fault—I hadn't taken steps to establish new friendships. Several acquaintances seemed willing, but I was holding back, hesitating....

As I studied the crazy quilt, I thought of the many friends I'd had throughout my life. Some felt a bit scratchy and rough like a sturdy piece of wool, but in time they softened—or I became used to them. Others were delicate like silk and needed to be handled with care. Some were colorful and bright and great fun to be with. A few special others felt soft and cozy like flannel, and they knew how to make me feel better.

Many of my friends have only been around for a season. So often I've had to leave them behind, or they leave me! And yet, in my heart, I know they are friends for life. If I met them on the street tomorrow, we would hug and laugh and talk nonstop. It would seem like yesterday.

And that's because God has sewn them into my heart.

I pulled the old quilt closer around me, comforted and warmed by my memories. Surely my own masterpiece—this quilt of friendships I fretted over—was not nearly finished. I would make new friends in this town. And like my great-grandmother, trusting her fingers to lead her, I would, by faith, reach out.

A friend is...
Someone who understands your past
Believes in your future
And accepts you just the way you are.

AUTHOR UNKNOWN

The Song

I breathed a song into the air,

It fell to earth

I know not where...

And the song,

from beginning to end,

I found again

in the heart of a friend.

HENRY WADSWORTH LONGFELLOW

May Basket of Flowers—and Forgiveness

Sue Dunigan

"Hey, do you know what? Today is May Day!" my sister announced. "Do you remember the May Day baskets we used to make with colored paper and paste?"

Childhood memories and warm feelings engulfed me as I recalled that my sisters and I would run around our neighborhood delivering the not-so-perfect baskets brimming with spring flowers. We would place the handmade treasures on a doorstep, knock on the door, then scurry away as fast as our legs could carry us. It was delightful to peer around a bush and watch our friends open their doors and pick up the colorful gift, wondering who had left it for them.

I distinctly remember the May Day of the year that I was in fifth grade. That year I was faced with a challenge involving one of my dearest friends. She lived right across the road from our family, and we had walked together to school nearly every day since first grade.

Pam was a year older than I, however, and her interests were starting to change from the interests that we had had together. A new family had recently moved into our small town, and Pam was spending more and more time at their house. I felt hurt and left out.

When my mother asked me if I was going to take a May Day basket to Pam's house, I responded angrily, "Absolutely not!" My mom stopped what she was doing, knelt down, and held me in her arms. She told me not to worry, that I would have many other friends throughout my lifetime.

"But Pam was my very best friend ever," I cried.

Mom smoothed back my hair, wiped away my tears, and told me that circumstances change and people change. She explained that one of the greatest things friends can do is to give each other a chance to grow, to change, and to develop into all God wants them to be. And sometimes, she said, that would mean that friends would choose to spend time with other people.

She went on to say that I needed to forgive Pam for hurting me—and that I could act out that forgiveness by giving her a May Day basket.

It was a hard decision, but I decided to give her a basket. I made an extraspecial basket of flowers with lots of yellow because that was

Pam's favorite color. I asked my two sisters to help me deliver my basket of forgiveness. As we watched from our hiding place, Pam scooped up the flowers, pressed her face into them, and said loudly enough for us to hear, "Thank you, Susie! I hoped you wouldn't forget me!"

That day I made a decision that changed my life: I decided to hold my friends tightly in my heart, but loosely in my expectations of them, allowing them space to grow and to change—with or without me.

God never loved me in so sweet a way before.

'Tis He alone who can such blessings send.

And when His love would new expressions find,

He brought thee to me and He said—

"Behold a friend."

AUTHOR UNKNOWN

If instead of a gem or

even a flower,

we should cast the gift

of rich thought

into the heart of a friend,

that would be giving

as the angels give.

GEORGE MACDONALD

Friendship Is a Diamond

Friendship is a diamond

buried in the earth;

a treasure of great worth.

But first it must be mined

then faceted and shined.

It takes pick and shovel and strain,

encompassing time and enduring pain,

until its grace is seen;

a glittering gift of love

that's shared between we three:

First God,

and you,

then me.

SALLY J. KNOWER

The Love Squad

Virelle Kidder

"Oh, no! Not company!" I groaned the moment my car rounded the corner and our house came into full view. Usually I'd be thrilled to see four cars lined up in our driveway, but after I spent a weeklong vigil at the hospital with an ill child, my house was a colossal mess. Turning off the car engine, I dragged myself to the front door.

"What are you doing home so soon?" my friend Judie called from the kitchen. "We weren't expecting you for another hour! We thought we'd be long gone before you got home." She walked toward me and gave me a hug, then asked softly, "How are you doing?"

Was this my house? Was I dreaming? Everything looked so clean. Where did these flowers come from?

Suddenly more voices, more hugs. Lorraine, smiling and wiping beads of perspiration from her forehead, came up from the family room where she had just finished ironing a mountain of clean clothes. Regina peeked into the kitchen, having finished vacuuming rugs and polishing and dusting furniture in every room in the house. Joan, still upstairs wrestling with the boys' bunk-bed sheets, called down her "hello," having already brought order out of chaos in all four bedrooms.

"When did you guys get here?" was my last coherent sentence. My tears came in great heaving waves. "How come...how come...you did all this?" I cried unashamedly, every ounce of resistance gone.

I had spent the week praying through a health crisis, begging God for a sense of His presence at the hospital. Instead, He laid a mantle of order, beauty, and loving care into our home through these four "angels."

"You rest a while, Virelle," Lorraine said firmly. "Here's your dinner for tonight—there are more meals in the freezer." The table was set with flowers and fancy napkins, and a little gift was at my place. A small banquet was arranged, complete with salad and dessert.

"Don't you worry. We're all praying," my friends said. "God has everything under control."

After my friends left, I wandered from room to room, still sobbing from the enormity of their gift of time and work. I found beautiful floral arrangements in every room...and little wrapped gifts on each bed. More tears.

In the living room I found a note under a vase filled with peonies. I was to have come home and found it as their only identity: "The Love Squad was here."

And I *knew* that God had everything under control.

One of the most beautiful qualities of true friendship is to understand and to be understood.

AUTHOR UNKNOWN

Amy Days

Lisa Latham Green

I've known Amy since kindergarten. She's been my best friend since second grade. Amy taught me long division. We were confirmed at the same time and were attendants at each other's weddings one summer. We went to graduate school and even bought our first houses simultaneously—houses with similar gigantic Los Angeles mortgages.

Through letters we kept tabs on our hopes and dreams, and when I learned of her pregnancy through a Christmas card, I immediately called to tell her of mine. We'd both been afraid to phone our news—afraid of somehow crushing the other with our good fortune.

I was due twenty-five days before Amy, committed to natural childbirth the Bradley way. Amy had chosen Lamaze. When she called me on the day before my due date, I said that I was in labor and it was sweet of her to call and check on me. She softly replied that she was calling to announce the birth of her daughter, Rebecca Anne, the day before.

Emily Catherine was born the following day, making our first children both girls, born two days apart. Emily's christening, an intimate affair including Amy and her tiny family, was scheduled a month later. It was the first time we'd seen each other in over two months. Amy had lost her baby weight. I hadn't. Since Amy had a few months before she had to return to work, she suggested that we get together. I agreed and called the next day. Thus began my "Amy Days."

Amy Days were special. They were canceled only for illness. Weekly, we alternated driving the thirty-two miles in Los Angeles traffic—one-and-a-half hours one way, but it was worth it. On Amy Days the dishes and laundry waited until I returned. I left with a light heart, a full diaper bag, and a smile. I would return, exhausted from the drive (about half an hour from home, Emily and I would get stuck in a traffic jam that usually provoked her to cry the rest of the way), but I would be renewed, ready to tackle the next week of mothering.

We planned outings to the library, buggy rides around our neighborhoods, photo sessions with still and video cameras, and excursions to the mall for makeovers. We designed matching Christmas playsuits, carefully sewing to fit our growing babies. But mostly we just played with our children and talked.

My husband's job has taken us to Austin, Texas, fifteen hundred miles from Amy, but we still stay in touch. Through phone calls, Amy and I have shared the scariness of bronchitis, the trials of potty training, and the joy we have in our blossoming children. And though my Amy Days are now mere phone calls at odd hours, they are no less important to the fabric of my life.

The Story of the Praying Hands

Author unknown

About 1490 two young friends, Albrecht Dürer and Franz Knigstein, were struggling young artists. Since both were poor, they worked to support themselves while they studied art.

Work took so much of their time and advancement was slow. Finally, they reached an agreement: they would draw lots, and one of them would work to support both of them while the other would study art. Albrecht won and began to study, while Franz worked at hard labor to support them. They agreed that when

Albrecht was successful he would support Franz, who would then study art.

Albrecht went off to the cities of Europe to study. As the world now knows, he had not only talent but also genius. When he had attained success, he went back to keep his bargain with Franz. But Albrecht soon discovered the enormous price his friend had paid. For as Franz worked at hard manual labor to support his friend, his fingers had become stiff and twisted. His slender, sensitive hands had been ruined for life. He could no longer execute the delicate brush strokes necessary to fine painting.

Though his artistic dreams could never be realized, he was not embittered but rather rejoiced in his friend's success.

One day Dürer came upon his friend unexpectedly and found him kneeling with his gnarled hands intertwined in prayer, quietly praying for the success of his friend although he himself could no longer be an artist. Albrecht Dürer, the great genius, hurriedly sketched the folded hands of his faithful friend and later completed a truly great masterpiece known as *The Praying Hands.*

Today art galleries everywhere feature

Albrecht Dürer's works, and this particular masterpiece tells an eloquent story of love, sacrifice, labor, and gratitude. It has reminded multitudes world around of how they may also find comfort, courage, and strength.

If there has come to us the miracle of friendship;
if there is a soul to which our soul has been drawn,
it is surely worthwhile being loyal and true.

HUGH BLACK

It is my joy in life to find
At every turning of the road
The strong arms of comrade kind
To help me onward with my load;
And since I have no gold to give,
And love alone must make amends,
My only prayer is, while I live—
God make me worthy of my friends.

FRANK DEMPSTER SHERMAN

My Forever Friend

Eva Marie Everson

I treasure an old black-and-white photograph framed in polished brass that sits on my dresser. The picture remains as crisp in detail as the year it was taken—1958. I'm no more than a year old, sitting in a stroller. Carla is clad in diapers and a T-shirt, force-feeding me from a Coke bottle. She's two years old and my best friend.

As girls we were inseparable. Our love for comic book heroes and teen magazines was rivaled only by our passion for swimming. Like the littlest of mermaids, we glided through the cold, blue water of the local pool, had "tea parties" on the floor of the shallow end, and dove for coins dropped in the deep end.

We snacked on peanut butter bars and hamburger pickles.

I survived asthma, and Carla survived cystic fibrosis.

During our teens, we comforted each other through the pains of becoming women and giggled over boys we later double-dated.

We took water ballet classes my sixteenth summer, but surgery forced me to drop out. Carla dropped out too. "Without you there," she told me, "it just wasn't the same."

After graduation we both chose to study nursing at the same school. Carla was my maid of honor at my wedding. She eloped, but in my heart, I stood beside my friend when she said her vows.

We're in our forties now. There are two states, four hundred miles, and six hours that separate us. But that's all that will ever come between us. Neither time nor distance will ever break our bond of friendship.

Nothing fades the photograph.

FRIEND is a present you give yourself—

That's one of my old-time songs—

So I put you down with the best of them

For you're where the best belongs.

Among the gifts I have given to me

Most comforting tried and true,

The one that I oftenest think about

Is my gift to myself of You.

CARRIE JACOBS BOND

I thank my God
every time I remember you.

PHILIPPIANS 1:3